WITHOUT ASKING

WITHOUT ASKING

poems

Jane Ransom

Winner of the 1989 Nicholas Roerich Poetry Prize

Story Line Press | *Pasadena, CA*

Without Asking

ISBN 978-1-58654-068-5 (tradepaper)
      978-1-58654-086-9 (casebound)

The National Endowment for the Arts, the Los Angeles County Arts Commission, the Ahmanson Foundation, the Dwight Stuart Youth Fund, the Max Factor Family Foundation, the Pasadena Tournament of Roses Foundation, the Pasadena Arts & Culture Commission and the City of Pasadena Cultural Affairs Division, the City of Los Angeles Department of Cultural Affairs, the Audrey & Sydney Irmas Charitable Foundation, the Kinder Morgan Foundation, the Meta & George Rosenberg Foundation, the Allergan Foundation, the Riordan Foundation, Amazon Literary Partnership, and the Mara W. Breech Foundation partially support Red Hen Press.

Second Edition
Published by Story Line Press
an imprint of Red Hen Press
www.redhen.org

Acknowledgments

These poems originally appeared in the following publications: "The Neighbors Slept" (originally titled "Dreaming, then—") in *Nit & Wit*; "Judy" in *Passages North* and *Anthology of Magazine Verse Yearbook of American Poetry, 1986-1988*; "Visit" in *Violet*; "The Family" in *Sojourner*; "About Your Christmas Card Picturing You and Your Husband" in *Negative Capability*; "Hopeful Meeting with the Chemotherapy Patient" in *Pearl,* and "Sequence" in *Webster Review.*

Besides winning the 1989 Nicholas Roerich Poetry Prize, the poems in this book garnered a New York Foundation for the Arts fellowship, as well as residencies at the MacDowell and Yaddo artist colonies. Upon publication, *Without Asking* received widespread acclaim, including this praise in the *Literary Supplement* of the New York *Village Voice*:

Journalist Ransom's first collection of poems is like a sheaf of homunculus short stories. The scale is an inch to a mile, but these poems leave out nothing you could ask for in the best fiction: character, conflict, ambiguity, even plot. A couple of phrases and a metaphor do the work of whole chapters. Her subject is secrecy: an alcoholic father hides the empties "as if they were Easter eggs," a lonely, terrifying brother throws his 13-year-old sister on the bed and begs her to make love with him. Recognizing that early pain can have complicated consequences, Ransom replaces self-pity with sympathy, anger, and honesty.

FOR MY MOTHER, SHIRLEY F. STATON
1929–1988

Contents

III

WITHOUT ASKING

Preface

Soon after *Without Asking* won the 1989 Nicholas Roerich Poetry Prize, I began to rebel against Confessionalism. I felt that my book (along with Confessional poetry in general) presented the "I" of the author as both hero and victim in a manipulative bid for readers' approval. Meanwhile, being at that time intrigued by postmodern philosophy, I sought to bypass the problem by shifting from narrative to so-called nonnarrative verse. Thus, my second poetry book took a wild turn away from the mainstream.

Or at least that's a possible explanation of what transpired after this first book came out. On the other hand, you could say that having grown bored with one form of expression, I sought the excitement of trying another. That also would be true.

And the impulse didn't stop there. Before even finishing the second poetry volume, *Scene of the Crime*, I rebelled against it as well, returning to narrative but switching to fiction and writing a novel, *Bye-Bye*. Intellectually, I was falling out of love with postmodernism. Emotionally, I'd discovered that if a poet plays too hard to get, she'll end up alone, and I felt lonely.

Following publication of those three books, it struck me that, despite their aesthetic differences, all three were a form of navel-gazing, ego-driven, show-offery. This isn't to say I was ashamed of my work. The fact that it had been indeed *work*—labor-intensive, disciplined, and aiming for excellence—made me proud. But stubbornly gazing inward had become for me a dead end or worse, a descent into alienation. I wasn't happy. I began studying how to change and how to help others change too. I opened a coaching office. Over time, I wrote a nonfiction book on the science of change, *Self-Intelligence*.

Throughout my zig-zags from one sort of book to another, a few constants emerge. The most obvious is a fascination with the self. (What is the self? What shapes the self? How can the self transform the self? Etc.) But something else stands out to me now, in the poetry books especially. Re-reading these poems, I recognize a protracted endeavor to not-need God—along with a contradictory objection to the supposed absence of God... as well as the yearning to be loved by God in all my terrible humanity.

Just to clarify: as people go, I'm pretty nice. But I'm also incurably human.

Finally, after decades of blindly bashing my head against the maze of self-important suffering, I looked up and there, to my astonishment, was God. More recently, and more shocking to me (having grown up among atheists, and having long looked down on Christians, in particular), there was Jesus—not the Church, but simply Jesus, incarnation of God's perfect love.

I believe that many paths lead to what or whom we might call God. I believe that God, being fully Other, cannot be contained by human language, nor by any religion, much less by my personal choice of paths. Moreover, to declare I've become a follower of Jesus is to speak yet again of (among, admittedly, many things) my *self*, in its inherent limitedness.

For me, God delineates the self while simultaneously expanding the self by crossing its boundaries. Or you could just say, Jesus rescued me. That also would be true.

In one of the poems here, I wrote that God "visits the lonely, like a stray dog." Despite that cheap line, and my youthful effort to scorn faith, God refused to reject me. Gradually it has become clear that it was I who was both "the lonely" *and* the stray creature attempting—and failing—to be self-sufficient.

In the book's penultimate poem, entitled "Conviction," I wrote, "I will meet the fish. After dinner tonight / the candles expose its track of bones. / There is no baptism to save me." In the last lines of the book's subsequent and final poem, entitled "Becoming a Fish," I wrote, "We are flying / through the Devil's house. / He is innocent."

Both poems are well wrought. Both are honest. They announce a voluntary passage into the unknown, a laudable willingness to risk being "bad" in pursuit of truth, and a rejection of any neat dichotomy separating evil from good. However, I think they also convey a defensive misunderstanding about God, an assumption that God prefers antiseptic piety. I now think God loves us exactly as we are—in all our human imperfection. Thus loved, we can hope to change.

Otherwise, looking inward may too easily lead to despair. One morning several years ago I began pulling volumes at random from the 20th-century poetry books on my shelves and letting the pages fall open. Nearly every poem was a protest, a refusal, a cry against our world. The preponderance of pain startled me, but it shouldn't have, given the number of modern writers who've committed suicide, and given that of course I'd read all those poems before. I had once felt deeply drawn to such artistic anguish. I thought it brave. But I now see it's also cowardly, a form of hiding in the shadows to protect the ego.

There's beauty in this first book, yet also fear masked as courage. Can I—or you, or any human—ever break completely free of fear? Maybe not. Yet we can evolve toward something greater than ourselves. If friendly aliens arrive on Earth tomorrow to tell me I'm mistaken about Jesus, I hope to ask good questions. The truer my faith, the less likely—and less afraid—I am to change my mind.

If ever I return to writing verse, it will be a poetics of joy, of a self facing inward and outward in communion with what is and may be. Recently, preparing for a cross-country move, I downsized my book collection, keeping only the most precious. One of those is *Leaves of Grass*, wherein Walt Whitman sings, "Do I contradict myself? Very well, then I contradict myself, I am large, I contain multitudes."

—Jane Ransom, 2019

I

Knowledge

I am the girl in her father's closet,
braiding ties, filling shoes
with marbles and beetle skins.
I squat with my knees up
against my chin, humming and dreaming
of Mommy's hands—the way they pinch
an unbaked crust
into a round collar of ruffles.
Our house is square, and brown
as a sea-sized puddle. This summer
the chimney, thrusting up like a periscope,
pulls the outside in.
When I look, my face turns dark.
Dog whistles
through the O of a steak bone
as she clicks by, bone on wood,
to a basement burial ground.
Her sounds mask mine, and I become
the girl in the closet who cannot look
away but sees the tie
drop and shoes fall, their feet swinging up
to where I've ridden on my daddy's neck.
I am the one stuck where I am
at the closet crack, suddenly silent
and still as the house itself,
breathing with my eye.

The Bottles

For years I routed them out,
avidly, as if they were Easter eggs,
from cabinet corners and beneath pillows.
I caught each one off-guard,
asleep like a soldier in his brown bag.
In my closet they stood like Russian troops
wearing stiff, icy coats.
They gathered strength in numbers
and I grew afraid,
knowing underneath such gray complexions
their blood ran hot and cold as the Devil's.
On the night I left, there were nearly a hundred,
gleaming confidently in my flashlight.
They clanked against each other
as I lined them up on the kitchen table
where they could salute my father
whenever he awoke, and raised his head.

Visit

Like an old mule's spine,
the oak support bent more each year,
till the porch fell in a heap of joints and limbs.
From its back this morning I must step far up to the door,
as if your "Little Calamity" again.
The house, too, sinks steadily lower,
a cart abandoned where the mule stopped pulling.
The floor thickens with cockroaches and mold
even now as you serve soot-flecked eggs
at the table where we sit, talking almost
as do other fathers and daughters,
me praising how thin you slice the bread, as if you didn't
last year twist this knife
so that the blade wavered
like a poplar leaf: dark, then light.
Your right eye twitched like a firefly
as you stood, swaying
before me:
"Maybe I'll kill you."

He Looks Like My Father

And so I try to crawl backward,
squeezing small enough to fall through his eye—
his sea, flecked with gold bubbles and green sequins
and go deeper, into the liquids below,
as if he were woman, and had a womb.
I search his lips
for blood-reds of childhood—
my skinned knees, my first menstruation—
and his tongue buds for the starfish
sidling beneath me,
as I dog-paddled the Mediterranean.

Dreaming of Father

The sun gathers itself
into a red disk, is pushed
through its slot.
Like a businessman
after work, the night drops its white shirt
and glides, naked, into my bed.
Man-not-my-father,
when we wake together, I am heavy
with love; it lies
over me—a down cover,
hot and tranquilizing.
The night undid me.
So large it pinned me in place.
So sharp it entered my mouth
tasting of my father's breath
when he bent down
to mark my forehead.
Now the night flies overhead—
a male witch,
his cape fixed with a bone button.

Instinctively, you kiss the spot
that he kissed. You say, "My sweet baby."

I curl my pale limbs
into a ball, and fall, without falling,
as the moon does. Yes,
it was a trick;
only my father was real,
and the kisses I give you
are his.

Training Our Filly on the Lunge Line

Dad, I crooked my wrist behind your knee.
I pressed the plumpness
of my cheek to the fist
of your hip. She strutted round us,
lowering her ears like jet wing-flaps,
aiming her nose at the hills, and pulling against her tether
as if she were a hooked fish.
As you turned with her, I turned with you.
The rope was a spoke; we were the hub. Her chest
shone damp as the bend in your leg, as she printed our wheel
in the clay. But just when I felt most-loved,
you reeled in the line,
to stroke her shuddering lips. She sucked salt
from your fingers, and you kissed beneath her ears.
She would stand motionless all night, content
for life, in her cubical stall. But I,
too, was her master, and so could forgive her,
while at home my sneer
made Mother wring her hands
as if love could be milked from the air.

For My Brother

We lit a driftwood pyre with your magnifying glass.
The roasting pinecone opened itself
like a mother's hand. We ate the flesh
of its seeds. Nearby
the Mediterranean ticked without stop
above the angelfish
while behind our cave, in the cliff-side house,
she placed a note in Father's typewriter:
I give up,
since you want me still and silent.
I believe the ink unfurled, frail as a spider,
when he smoothed out the sheet.
Then he crushed it
in his palm. Yes, I know, you and I had filled
our ears, like conch shells,
with noise. But no matter:
What happened next
we could not have stopped.

My Mother

You stood with back arched,
bony fingers breaking
stale bread into a bowl.
I sat behind you
in the breakfast nook,
my pendulous feet
swaying lethargically
as a wound-down clock.
I was pressing a knife
at a slant through a carrot;
the slices lay like many
jaundiced eyes.
The Formica table shimmered
river-green between us.
I told you how I was bleeding.
The clicking and scraping
of dinner-making filled
the kitchen forest.
You turned to me warily
as lioness toward human,
muscles coiling in your
shoulders and loins
before you edged closer—
and were stalking me
across hardwood; we were locked
in the bathroom. Then you were
her again, tearing the slab
of cotton from its box,
undoing the safety pins.

Reunion

for my mother

The air tastes sharp as green mangoes ripening inland,
whose pits will someday loosen into roots.
As we drift along the shore, I can't stop
swallowing, to free the stone in my throat.
I purse my lips in frustration and build a face
out of sand. You bend down, pat at
the cold, dry mouth
as if it might be coaxed to open,
a pearl on its tongue.

The Ice Doll

She was white as my mother's nightgown.
She was not clear. She was hard
as my brother's teeth, and did not bleed.
She wore my sailor dress. Stiffer than a paper cup,
it stuck to her like wax. She smiled pertly,
as if for my kindergarten photograph.
When you hold my breasts like this
your hands turn to hot stones.
Who are you to doubt my bedtime story?
As you press against us her dress
slips down, soaking your shirt. She grows
almost transparent then.
I see many dark objects inside her—
the doctor's bulging glove and
crotch; my father,
holding his wife's hands
at her sides, him saying,
"Do not move at all. That's right."

Halloween Papier-Mâché

We loved to tear apart grownups' lives, taking Great
from snot-ass Britain; removing the pope from his spaceship hat. We plunged
each strip of lies in sludge and slathered it to a balloon.
Our mother scanned the word patterns for revelation, as if flipping
through Bible pages or radio stations, willing to trust
some random adage. But those soppy phrases were nothing
to the stiff-eyed beast she'd become.

Home Alone at Age 12

Windows skim the ceiling.
A car is jerked up the gravel hill by the line of a sole headlight.
My right eye lies awake, tucked in its pink cradle.
The pupil twists on its tiny neck,
wresting shapes from the dark. The dogs sprawl on my floor,
wheezing through moist lips. I cry out,
and all three mutts scratch
across parquet, to where I wait,
pillow pushed between my knees. Then the dogs,
who love me, mother me. They mother me.

My Mother's Cotton Underwear

Spring, 1964

Though I'd dressed fast as I could, snatching clothes from the top
of the unsorted laundry wrinkled or not, knowing I was late
for school, still, on the way down our hill I paused
many times to look at the worms, sprinkled like pink confetti
against the rain-blackened asphalt. Also, it took a long time
to step from bare place to bare place without crushing any
of those beckoning fingers. So the driver was honking
and the others kids stared, as I took the turn onto the last stretch.
I ran toward the bus, my lunchbox banging my knees.
That's when they fell, white as a halo, around my feet.

Summer, 1970

When one poked its fleshy nose out from under its cover, I would tweak it off
and plop it into the aluminum basin that heated up enough
to burn my fingers, if I left it propped in the sun as I waddled backward
down the rows, my pincers moving out, and in, until my hands
overflowed. When I took the bowlfuls to her, my mother would say,
"How satisfying this is—and *always* will be, Dear." But that summer I was
getting my period and the boys were coming around.—I refused
to pick more strawberries.

Waking Up

On my thirteenth birthday, I see you standing
next to my bed, and realize that while 1 was sleeping, you entered
my room, and shut the door. "Jane, let's make love."
A clothesline coils in one hand,
brown nylon braid glistening
like a python out of its egg.
I stand up and feel smaller.
Gripping a handful of nightgown at my neck
the way boys clutch kittens to drop in the river,
you fling me back onto the bed,
and giggle at the lightness of my body.
"Because I love you, Jane." You fumble
with the rope. "I love you
too. Let's go outside. I need air."
I promise that I won't run away.
After all, I'm your sister—I'll help you,
you look so anxious. Confused,
you escort me out of my bedroom, across the den—
step by step, learning a dance together.
You undo the back door, guide me
onto the porch. You're winding
the chord around my wrists when I bolt
toward the neighbors' house
fast as a branded witch
escaping the stake, and the flames.

II

For My Mother

Like the twenty-ninth of February, it has returned. "Inoperable."
The word reverberates like aluminum nailed onto the shaft of your lung
which by now is so fragile the surgeons won't try
to scoop out the soft nugget glowing in the tired vein.
I've seen how a film-maker quickens the frames to make a rose bloom
and die in seconds. My stepfather went from groom to bald invalid
and vanished in a poof of ashes. All within a year. You remember
that I missed the wedding, as if to stop his fingers from leading your finger
through that hoop, your hands guiding his mouth to the fiery lipstick kiss
that said: It is done. But I bought flowers
the next winter, for his funeral. A purple bud thrusts its tip into the air
of your lung—and I watch, helpless as any audience.

Hopeful Meeting With
the Chemotherapy Patient

You had been waiting years for me
to greet you without holding back.
But I got off the plane in Charleston, the wrong city.
When at last, at 3 a.m., in my short red skirt,
I broke from the jet's umbilical cord
and strode into Savannah Airport, you stood up,
smaller than I remembered. Your face was shadowed
by a bouffant wig, yet the bald flanges
of your eyebrows gleamed, like razor clams
under water. That afternoon
while I half-slept on the sofa,
you placed your finger in my palm
the way grownups do to infants. I held on
as if you'd fallen through the ice—as if
I could save you.

Vacation on Hilton Head Island

Though it was smaller than the coin-sized crabs
molting in the mud slick, your tumor brought the family together that week.
We five leaned over the bridge, dropping breadcrust after breadcrust
to make the crabs throng into one greedy ball. Waving straw hats,
we threw shadows that drove them into their holes
like pills into a crowd of mouths. We muddied our feet in the swamp,
as if dipping fruit in chocolate, enclosing them in fragile casts.
We photographed sanderlings amassed in a tree like a cluster of boneset,
until all at once the blossoms unhinged; they drifted down as their claws,
black seeds, sought earth. In one pond stood a great blue heron,
its neck bent in the S of stillness, then straightening fast,
the beak splitting into a less-than sign, and closing around a mullet.
Our last day there we found the alligator, so small we laughed
when it raised its broadsword snout to the branch you shook.

Fitful Night in Indiana

Sam Spade, only male in the house, yawns
into my left instep, the yellow fur of his gullet dividing
then clenching like a sea anemone. He started the night purring
in the master bed, but Mother's coughing annoyed him,
and here was another warm body. There's the flutter
of her kimono. Now she's running
water in the sink. It doesn't cover the scalding
bursts of phlegm, being shot past the epiglottis,
into the drain. The door opens. The light quits. Our pupils
fatten again, as she feels her way to the bed's socket,
the filaments in her lung sputtering.

After Chemotherapy

I wind the scarf around your exposed scalp
as if covering a sunflower in gauze
to keep the sparrows off.
You kneel in the caterpillar grass,
gazing across this meadow that once held willows
and yellow lady's-slipper,
toward the dry bed of our creek.
When the ends of the silk have been crossed and twisted
like a tourniquet, I pin them in place.

What She Saw

Staring straight ahead,
her eyes were whirlpools pulling
her face under; her skin wrinkled
like water, unclinging from clavicles
sharp as dry vines. Only
the forehead jutted like a bank overhang.

I rubbed her gently, skimming over
the obtrusive branch of her spine,
massaging down the withered thighs
to the blue, swollen feet. I ran a wet finger
along her lips. And when she watched,

she watched not my hand,
but my eyes—glass bowls
where our deaths floated
like two clipped blossoms.

Did she see her own death
sending me flowers, did she witness
the petals coaxed open, delicately
bruised? Did she watch the truck pulling up
with its gloved driver? Did she glimpse the black tongues
of his shoes—or an impatiens' yellow skin?
Or had color given in to form, so that what she saw

was a pogonia's frilled labium, and scalloped edges
of the deliverer's fist.

Gently, I ran a wet finger along her lips.

And at last, after those had turned greenish-white,
I sat by my mother, holding her hand,
and watching the tight buds of her lids
for a dark, wet strip that erratically
wormed its way between her lashes.
Then she muttered: "Help"—or was it, "Hell."

Her lips shrunk back, her teeth emerged
like a prehistoric stone circle
and she cried out, "Lift me—please."

We lined up alongside her bed, my hands under
the calves so tender a thumbprint could last hours,
Fran raising her torso, and Farley hoisting
her shoulders and head. But finally,
though she said, "Higher. Please, higher—"
and stared straight ahead, we didn't know what she saw—
and we couldn't hold her much longer.

The End of the Vigil

Much of her had already escaped through the slats of molecules.
The brush-shaped hair, the bright clay
coloring of her face, even the lips
like squeezed-out-and-pinched-off
cylinders of acrylic Plum Red
had faded from the pale flatness
we'd come to call real.
Her soul may have wound around
or through us that February day—
or next year, time being
curved like glass bent
on reflecting itself.
Call it avoidance; I don't
know where she is "now" any more
than the place of the universe—
but I reconstruct
that night, her color and gloss
seeping out until her raised
translucent hand
striated the closely woven air
from throat to bedrail.

Epilogue

You can see the whites of her eyes, still
open to the flames that lap her skin like the warm
tongue of a St. Bernard. You don't understand. Death's nothing
to anyone by then—immaterial
as life is, as we are, though we lean over
the canister of ashes. It's generic
in stainless steel, shaped like a milk jug
brimming with light, the blood stains boiled out.
I breathe into its mouth. It breathes back
dust that sticks in the damp
corners of my eyes, like sleep. I could
give you a word for it, but it would be my word
as this is my grief. Here.
Take the color white.

III

About Your Christmas Card
Picturing You and Your Husband

I, too, could send you a photograph,
 a note from Manhattan. But when I look up
your address, the floor shudders
as hundreds of commuters pass below,
eyes opaque as envelopes, shoulders folded,
elbows flat, as if being mailed
to the door-slots of their homes.
Here the poinsettia extends her shriveling stalks,
while outside new snow leaves
the streets unglazed. The air
in this building exhausts itself,
the pipes squeak—dirty and intrusive, unlike
your body, as I imagine it.

In the mountains, the snow would not hold us.
We fell, and kissed. Your eyes teared,
your hand moved to touch my face. But I refused,
I stood up. Your eyelashes froze
and snapped, dark fragments of words. I will write,
"Dear Jo Ann—I remember our vows; I still love you.
You must know that." I will write it
in my journal. The sun descends with the snow.
The Earth reddens, and turns away.

Judy

As a girl, she unzipped milkweed pods,
peeled silky hairs from the shafts,
touched the thick milk.
She sat naked in the creek. Water
foamed through her fingers and knees.

This was before her breasts grew too fast
and drew sneers from the boys at recess;
before her father yelled
when she forgot to sit with knees shut
in a dress, and long before a man threw her
to the ground, saying he loved her.

Now she goes to the quarries with a group of women.
They take a German shepherd and a rifle.

They unbutton themselves
in the rock-washed water.

They loosen their laughs into the air—
laughs that climb
in backward waterfalls.

The Fashion Model

The bumpy, hairy potato
and the lopsided squash
envy the egg, as she
balances herself delicately,
one smoothly rounded oval
in her starched, white shell.
They feel jealous
when she's dyed pink,
or put primly in an egg cup,
her special pedestal.

Cindy

That night rain splunked against the snow
where it hardened like glossy paint,
and after Cindy stayed for dinner, my mother said
she couldn't go home, because the roads were slick.
So she sat on my rug, and I kneeled
behind her, braiding and smelling her hair.
Then we lay in my mother's double bed,
parallel and stiff as a pair of new shoes,
and I told her I could show her how Don Riley kissed
using thumbs and tongue both. But Cindy said no.
The next day we skated to the store,
and I made Cindy carry home the eggs. Almost
there, she hit a bump, spun around twice—
the white grocery bag lifting from her hand
like a startled bird—and landed with legs out
before her, and eggs safely tucked
in their carton in her lap. Immaculate.

With Gloria in San Juan

From the alley,
salsa rises, *toque*
por toque,
each note shoving
into its brother—
who is like
the one before it—aah, like
an incestuous lover: I can smell it,
I can smell her,
thrumming her hips, twisting her ribcage,
slithering iguana-like
under my hands; I can smell me,
oozing to the
thump of her knuckles, thump
of her thumbs—one hunching
after the other, muchacha, muchacha, muchacha.

(***toque***, tō'-kā, means drumbeat)

Without Asking

In the first place we were all alike,
tattooed nipples and libratory privates
beneath our habits. And no man touched us, not even Him.
We ate with our hands, tongued up the worms
of sizzled onions, dug for the roots
that thickened our stew. We knelt
before one another, to give ourselves
whatever we asked.

In the second, I divide and multiply my faith. Against kitchen walls,
we defy gravity—
lying on back and stomach at once
standing up. I worship the strangeness of others;
their mysteries glint in this light—bronze bells
where I see myself
distorted, and surrender to whatever
contracts and expands me. They sway, I am swayed
by the ringing of clouds, letting fall
the rains without asking.

The Dancers

They press palm against palm
and drift into each other
as if dancing through mirrors, to retrieve their bodies
from strangers. They don't turn back
to see her beneath him—how stiff
she lay, year after year, agreeing to it.
He is banished now. All those
unlike them are safe behind glass
to be pinned and studied and blamed for the pestilence
that must never again be let out of its box—
Pandora is not feared; she was maligned.
With fingers, they fashion themselves again and again,
molding breasts and labia like porcelain.
Perhaps Orpheus really was a woman. If so, like her,
they must save what they love,
and never look behind them.

The Neighbors Slept

Dreaming, then whiteness.
The house was surrounded
by moonlight. From twin beds,
each saw the other's irises.
The light drifted in;
it glistened on the sheets
like fresh snow. They donned nightclothes
and stumbled to the patio.
It shone silver. She waltzed
alone, in silence. Then he lifted his trombone
from its casket and launched bubbles that turned
gold and green and rose
to the parent globe.
Her nightgown glowed; it rippled.

Irazú

Even the plants worry me. These succulent
gold-veined leaves move too much for this breeze.
Clouds roll like sweat off the mountain as we pull ourselves to the top,
where the gorge tears open, its huge walls pleated
as the lining of a mushroom. And just as black—and soft.
I step back, knowing if I fall, my body will not return.
But you hike out to the highest ridge, placing between us
this canyon ringed with lava, and as motionless
as I am when you hold me on the edge
of climax. While this moment lasts
I see you waving, and want to yell:

Drop to all fours. Put your face to the ground.

(**Irazú** is a volcano in Costa Rica)

In the Blue Ridge Mountains

As oak-leaf skeletons rose like sleepy children
to be led away through the fluted ravine,
our tent ballooned like a sail and heaved
toward the precipice. We woke up often
to hear the icy crack of the axes
of leaves piled beneath our ground cloth. When I rolled over,
the bruise on my hip grew definite; my skin became paper
between the press and the spine-shaped etching
of eastern hemlock. Nothing but grayish blue
the next morning, as we folded back frozen netting
to gaze 15 miles west, 4,000 feet down
at some Virginia town, poor as Cinderella,
that last night had glittered, but now
lay nearly insensible, beneath haze
the color of wrist veins.

Sequence

I. In the Science Museum

Here are twelve fetuses, lined up in jars
more meticulously labelled
than Mother's jam. The ones on the far end are large;
their toes, like molluscs, stick to the glass.
The biggest one's elbows are pinned
snug as the wings of a roasting hen.
Their lids are sealed, like the eyes
of a muslin doll who once lay by my bed
in a cardboard cradle. But these
underwater gurus sit
with crossed limbs, and lowered chins,
offering us their genitals
as evidence.

II. Ginger Steps

The city bus skids toward the light.
I step in front of it
when the sign says "Walk." My umbrella bloats
and cracks. The dripping wings flap in vain. I go on.
I take responsible steps, carrying myself
like a hot supper dish.
At last I am there. The white-frocked miss
arranges me deftly as a maid sets table,
sliding my washed feet into silver holders.

III. Intact

The air moves across me in bathwater waves.
The nurses stop at my bed, gathering smiles,
pink water lilies that will close in the dark.
Here everyone loves me, and at home
I will be cared for like a sleepy infant.
When this calm drains from my blood,
I will not be demoralized
by my pocked vein, and emptiness.
Otherwise, I would have refrained
from this operation, and agreed to wait
for God, who visits the lonely, like a stray dog.

Family

When he tells her to be still, she is
as static as a patch of moss
that shudders only when a whitetail doe
crumples on the spot
and takes a second slug, shot
to finish the job.
When he pushes off her,
as a man pushes off
in a boat, by pressing both hands
on the dock, she lies awhile,
then rises
with her sleepwalker's arms splayed out,
and her children close in,
clacking swizzle sticks in Kool-Aid cups.
"Our Mother,"
she hears them praying,
and every day pours down a sky of molten tar.
As each darkness falls, the kids unclench their toys
and run from corner to wall. She yells for order,
she smacks their ears and mouths.

Thomas Johnson

I once saw my friend Tommy fit a firecracker
like a tampon, into a cat. The year I turned five
his dad stopped by to pick him up
from my birthday party. Mr. Johnson
gave each child a caramel sucker,
and said, "I see ice cream on your pants.
Are you a monkey that can't keep clean?"
Then by one wrist he lifted his son,
swung him inside the trunk of the car
and slapped the lid down, as if it were
the cover of a book he was going to burn.

The Question

Of Shatila and Burj el Barajneh, Lebanon, February 1987

In this 20-year-old photo, my collie's ears wipe my chin
as I pinch the fur on her chest into peaks of frosting.
How can they? Grip a dog's head the way you do a butternut squash
to tug it off the vine—and hit it, with a rock. Then the group of children uses a
razor to open a seam, the way you split the back of Raggedy Ann.
The stuffing bulges out. They tear away the hide. They poke a stick
through the muzzle, out the anus. They gather rags and braid them into faggots
that will burn longer, under the spit, than those nine trick candles
in my cake that year—I huffed and huffed
but they refused to die. The question is, how it is
that hundreds of men can be allowed
to seal the camps as tight as pursed lips, until each child's bones
nearly pierce the skin.

Wartime Photograph in Nicaragua

Juan's arm locks around the thigh of a 3-year-old
propped against his torso like a ventriloquist's mannequin.
Four other daughters line up
like billboards; only the sixth shifts
in Angelita's womb. I'm an American
so when I say Freeze, he does. They all do.
His rifle, hanging from his shoulder,
rubs against his daughter's chest.
I back up and squeeze down.

In Jinotega Province

Nicaragua

Mud sucks the campesina's toes
as if they were sow's teats. The hogs and cows
on this farm are dead. She thinks
that the men who work for dollars
must have left this valley
before dawn. No one here now
but her five children in the beanfield.
Black and crisp as roasted apples,
their corpses hiss at the pellets of rain.

In Puebla, Mexico

for Luís

Sun polishes the cobblestone promenade. Hours yet
till someone sets glowing the streetlamps' white gumballs.
A clocktower rises over the stone mercado.
Its eye watches your arrival. Inside,
the walls are dark, cold as lizards. Their breath slides
into your clothes. You refuse to cry out,
running your finger along lips
of glazed jugs. You gaze at tied-up chickens
piled in heaps, like dirty laundry to be bleached,
except that their heads writhe.
The flower stalls hold ample wreathes
for a funeral. The fleshy, sweating butcher has blades
and appetite for slaughter. You turn your back on the birds.
You've come for the varnished, papier-mâché masks
that you've heard contain dead spirits.
You see your late father's face on the head of a goat.
For five pesetas, you will own his soul.

The Dead

I used to see the dead
pulling toward me
as arms
pull into the body, as long hair
stops flying, is sucked
to the shoulders.
And when I spoke
for them, I was like an infant
speaking for my mother
and father, in an infant's language
that over time is extinguished,
the way the light
eye-syrup of the dead
stiffens to agate.—Finally I've learned
they are separate
and disobedient.

Conviction

The fish man cuts off its head,
flings out its guts with a knife.
He bundles the body in white.
Down Tenth Street it rocks,
tucked in my bike basket.
Bathing in wine under the broiler,
its operculum expands and deflates,
breathing steam as if it were water.
These nights I lie on cold, bleached sheets,
roll into my pillow
and travel far from our life.
I will meet the fish. After dinner tonight
the candles expose its track of bones.
There is no baptism to save me.

Becoming a Fish

I thought I could breathe here.
Water is sweeter than oxygen.
I most feared the pressure
would stop me from speaking.
His legs grip my sides
like a vice; I have given in.
Rays whip their tails and arc
into comets. We are flying
through the Devil's house.
He is innocent.

Biographical Note

Jane Ransom is the author of two poetry volumes, one novel, and the non-fiction book *Self-Intelligence: The New Science-Based Approach for Realizing Your True Potential.* Her first poetry book, *Without Asking,* won the Nicholas Roerich poetry prize. Her novel, *Bye-Bye,* won the Mamdouha S. Bobst Award. She has been awarded residencies at Yaddo and MacDowell artist colonies in the United States, and at Fundación Valparaíso in Spain. She's the recipient of poetry fellowships from the New York Foundation for the Arts and the Massachusetts Cultural Council. A former international news editor and writing professor, Jane Ransom has taught at Rutgers University and New York University, and as the Distinguished Poet in Residence at St. Mary's College in Moraga, CA. She now serves as a speaker and trainer on brain plasticity and the science of personal transformation. Using her Self-Intelligence® model, she coaches individuals for a growth mindset and helps organizations to improve leadership and employee engagement. A native Midwesterner, she has lived in New York, Boston, Madrid, Paris, San Juan (Puerto Rico), and San Francisco, before moving to Durham, North Carolina.